Introduction..

15 Best Indoor Gardening Ideas ....

   Creative Indoor Gardening Ideas..

      1. Hanging Terrarium Indoor Gardening 4

      2. Moss Ball Indoor Gardening (Kokedama) 6

      3. Custom Large Pot Indoor Gardening 6

      4. Vertical Gardening 8

      5. Pallet Basket Hanger Indoor Gardening 10

      6. Hover Dishes Indoor Gardening Idea...10

      7. Wooden Drawers Indoor Gardening 11

      8. Mini herb Terrarium Indoor Gardening 12

      9. Suspended Indoor DIY Vertical Garden 13

      10. Creative Pipe Indoor Gardening 14

      11. Hanging Kitchen Organizer Indoor Garden 15

      12. Simple Potted Indoor Garden 16

      13. IKEA Utility Cart Indoor Gardening 17

      14. DIY Tabletop Indoor Gardening Terrarium 19

      15. Tiered Cake Stand Indoor Gardening...21

   Indoor Gardening Advices & Tricks 23

      Space 23

      Ventilation and the Seasons 28

      Indoor Herb Gardening..38

      Indoor Vegetable Gardening 40

   Indoor Gardening Supplies 44

      Culture Lights 44

      Window Garden Kits 44

      Hydroponic Indoor Gardening System 45

   Indoor Gardening Frequently Asked Questions 45

      Is indoor gardening hard?..45

      May you implement indoor gardening with a vegetable garden? 46

      When may I start indoor gardening? 46

   Final Thoughts on Indoor Gardening 46

Introduction

In this book, you will see 15 ideas for home gardening.

Most people like herbs, however not everyone has the right resources or space to start up a garden. however culturing herbs doesn't have to be limited to a place.

You can always culture herbs indoors. Instead of doing an outdoor yard, you can opt for indoor gardening.

15 Best Indoor Gardening Ideas

Don't have a patch of ground to herb things in? No problem! **Indoor gardening** offers an excellent introduction to the wonderful world of gardening. Whether you're a gardening novice or pro, whether you live in a tiny flat or big house, you can find lots of ideas and inspiration in this article.

Most people like herbs, however not everyone has the right resources or space to start up a garden. however culturing herbs doesn't have to be limited to a place.

You can always culture herbs indoors. Instead of doing an outdoor yard, you can opt for **indoor gardening**.

Indoor gardening caters to a lot of people, from the inexperienced up to the experts. Granted, there are a couple of things you must to consider, however we'll touch on them later.

For now, let's explore along some of the best indoor gardening ideas around.

Creative Indoor Gardening Ideas

Anyone may do **indoor gardening**, regardless of their skill level. A beginner may culture a spectacular yard, however knowing a thing or two about herbs can make the entire process smoother.

Our list focuses on easy indoor gardening ideas that anyone may try right now.

1. Hanging Terrarium Indoor Gardening

Hanging terrariums are fairly simple to set up; you can only must a succulent or an climate herb and a glass bowl.

They take up little to no space, making them perfect for places with very little area to spare!

2. Moss Ball Indoor Gardening (Kokedama)

The *kokedama* is a Japanese moss ball, also called the poor man's bonsai, that allows you to culture terrestrial herbs in a ball.

You can make this bigger or smaller depending on the plant. this looks great as this is or hung!

3. Custom Large Pot Indoor Gardening

You can culture a garden in a pot outside or indoors. This idea lets you go wild with your garden ideas on a small scale.

You can even go ahead and put props like a fairy garden kit or creative rocks in it. In the example above, the pot is cleverly broken for a good effect.

4. Vertical Gardening

Vertical gardening is a handy indoor gardening idea that doesn't take up much space and may simply be adapted to your needs.

This one's perfect for an indoor herb garden. It's perfect for blank walls or windows, and you can even go ahead and employ the herbs for cooking!

5. Pallet Basket Hanger Indoor Gardening

This is one more kind of vertical indoor gardening and more of a DIY and recycling method than the one above.

Wooden pallets are easy to find; you can go to a nearby warehouse and ask for them. You can adapt them to your space and besides, they are environmentally friendly.

6. Hover Dishes Indoor Gardening Idea

Hover dishes are as what its name suggests, a dish that hovers and hangs on a steel wire. You can buy readymade hover dishes from online indoor gardening websites, or simply make your own.

A shallow dish and a several succulents would suffice for a DIY hover dish.

7. Wooden Drawers Indoor Gardening

Herbs are usually small herbs. So they are perfect for being potted inside wooden drawers.

Supposing you have a spare drawer lying around, you can employ this to Make an environmentally friendly indoor herb <u>garden</u> while also adding a vintage feel to your space.

8. Mini herb Terrarium Indoor <u>Gardening</u>

Mini herb terrariums are perfect tabletop designs. Some indoor gardening stores sell ready-made mini terrariums, however some also offer customized terrariums, where you can take the design and the terrarium herbs.

Of course, you can also go ahead and make your own terrarium.

9. Suspended Indoor DIY Vertical Garden

This is one more type of vertical indoor gardening that requires some handyman skills. Setting this up in the house needs some DIY skills, so ask help supposing you're not confident.

The end product has a clean aesthetic, and this saves space!

10. Creative Pipe Indoor Gardening

This is a pretty creative indoor gardening idea that takes advantage of a blank wall and some pipes you have lying around.

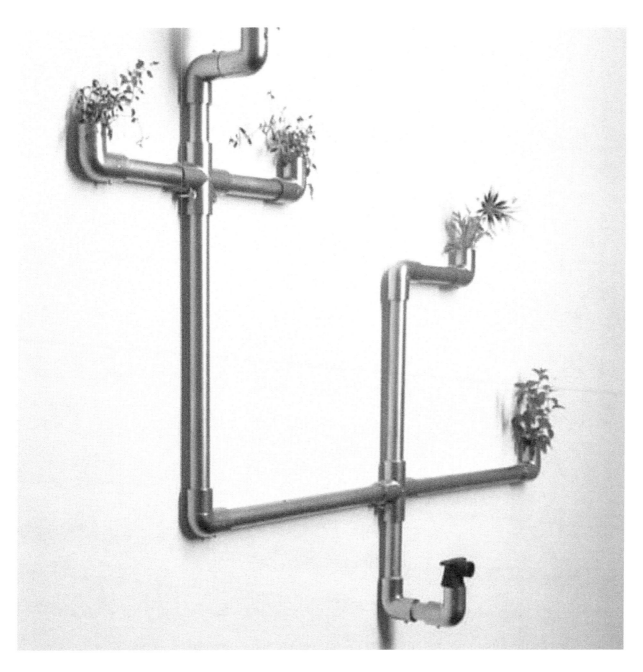

This is best used with herbs or other small herbs. It's a loveliness addition to a wide wall that needs a bit of life.

11. Hanging Kitchen Organizer Indoor Garden

Your hanging kitchen organizer possibly recycled into an indoor herb garden. Here's an example to see what we mean.

This design exudes that DIY feel that you might want to have around!

12. Simple Potted Indoor Garden

A lot of herbs possibly simply potted, making the potting method the easiest and most beginner-friendly indoor [gardening](#) idea.

For smaller spaces, you can opt for small pots like this above, however supposing you want something with more personality, go for a bigger pot with an equally larger plant.

13. IKEA Utility Cart Indoor Gardening

This is an IKEA utility cart filled with lots of different types of succulents; in essence, a succulent garden on wheels.

This possibly a temporary placeholder for your succulents as you prepare their place in the house, or you can simply allow this be like that permanently.

14. DIY Tabletop Indoor *Gardening* Terrarium

This is like a mini terrarium, however instead of being a tabletop design, the tabletop has become the terrarium itself!

It's a braver choice and a permanent design compared to the mini terrarium.

15. Tiered Cake Stand Indoor [Gardening](#)

There are cakes on a cupcake stand, and there are also succulents on a two-tier stand.

This is a perfect addition on a tabletop and since they're succulents, they must little attention for them to flourish.

Indoor Gardening Advices & Tricks

We shared with you a lot of ideas to inspire you to Make your own indoor garden. however before you get started, you may want to check our advices and tricks based on what you want to grow.

Plants culture best in their natural habitats. Therefore, to be able to culture herbs inside, you can must to replicate their optimal conditions indoors.

Most of the time, herbs are forgiving and they can thrive under normal indoor conditions, however some of them are more finicky, and you must to consider their needs.

Space

One of the main reasons for culturing an indoor garden is the lack of space to culture one outside.

You can bring the garden inside; no matter how much space you have available, indoor gardening can be there to slip into your life and house.

Most people who are into indoor gardening are this who want fresh produce right in their reach. In this context, the perfect spot to put an indoor garden is the kitchen, especially near the windows.

One more option is to employ hanging planters to Make a hanging indoor garden near the windows.

Indoor Gardening in Apartments

Apartments generally have small spaces right from the start, and having furniture doesn't help, either.

Potted herbs take very little of your functional space, and hanging ones even less. Plus, the visual result is good.

A study desk with a lot of herbs possibly a calming place to work and study.

A dash of green when you're feeling stressed may relax you and act as your destressing medicine.

Plus, indoor [gardening](#) lets you breathe in the fresh climate even supposing you are inside your house.

Indoor Gardening the Kitchen

Often, the best place to put your indoor yard, and especially herbs, is the kitchen. You can conveniently reach the herbs or veggies whenever you must them. Plus, the greenery can liven up the kitchen.

With indoor gardening in your kitchen, your herbs don't have to be separate from your utensils; they may coexist peacefully, as long as you keep your planters clean.

In this scenario, your herbs may hang along with your kettle, and you would have saved space as well as made some for your herbs!

Indoor Gardening in Containers

What about the other rooms? You can do indoor container gardening in simply about any room, though in dark rooms you may must to install culture lights.

With a several recyclable containers or store-bought ones, you can Make an indoor garden with no fuss.

Some containers must to be attached to one place, however many of them possibly moved anywhere you want at any time.

Ventilation and the Seasons

Not all herbs culture all year round. Some culture best in summer conditions, while some culture their flowers sooner than others.

While with indoor gardening you don't have to worry about the weather, you still must to factor in the seasons and the role they play in your herbs' development.

Summer

Many herbs take the summer very well. Summer provides them the right amount of hours in the sun and temperature for them to grow.

You must put your herbs near windows where they'll receive enough sun and heat for them to thrive. Supposing you can, you can also move them outside to allow them enjoy the warm and bright light.

Fall

Fall is the season of falling leaves, and flowers in shades of yellow and orange are perfect for this season. The conditions are still right to culture quite a several herbs, so take advantage of that.

For an autumn feel, getting flowers and herbs in the color palette of orange and yellow can definitely make your house look great.

Advice: Remember that you can culture herbs and certain vegetables pretty much all-year-round with the right gardening kit.

Winter

Supposing summer is the happy season of gardening, winter must be the bane of gardening. There's the very little sun, and the cold is not something that herbs love, though some of them actually must it.

But this is also at this time that indoor gardening shows its advantages.

Gardening during winter is best done indoors, with the help of culture lights. Culture lights compensate for the cold temperatures and little sun, letting your herbs culture in optimal conditions no matter the season.

Despite the cold, you can force flowers to have a winter bloom. The ways to do this can vary across flowers, however this is definitely doable.

Spring

Springtime is the season when everything starts to culture back from the winter. You can definitely get some flowers and allow them thrive happily on your tabletops as part of your indoor [gardening](#) activities!

Force-blooming some off-season flowers are one of the joys of indoor gardening. Simply like the winter bloom, you also must to prep the bulb before you can get some good flowers inside in springtime.

Indoor Herb Gardening

Indoor gardening with herbs is easy, making this perfect for beginners. Since herbs are typically small, you have a lot of flexibility and plenty of design choices.

The biggest benefit of culturing your own herbs inside is the convenience and freshness of the herbs. You have your herbs within arm's reach and they're fresh and fragrant.

Herbs are fairly easy to grow. There are three things to consider when doing indoor gardening with herbs: temperature, drainage, and placement.

Advice: Temperature is less of a problem than with other types of herbs since herbs culture fine in an indoor environment.

You also must to be mindful of drainage because you wouldn't want your herbs' roots to rot in water.

Placement in the house matters when this comes to herb gardening. Herbs must as much natural sun as they may get, and they usually get this near windows.

Advice: Keep herbs for at least 6 hours in the sun.

Because herbs are small, you can put them in jars like these then have them tightly placed on wooden planks. You may also want to put labels on your herbs.

It possibly convenient to have these herbs in the kitchen so that you can snip them at the moment you must them.

This is a vintage herb garden made employing a free wall and some metal buckets. It's a bigger herb yard, and this looks pretty neat, too.

Indoor Vegetable Gardening

Vegetable gardening doesn't have to end in winter. When the outside gets too cold or when you simply don't have "the outside," you can migrate your vegetables inside and culture them there.

Given that some vegetables are stocky herbs that are more outdoorsy than herbs, culturing them inside can be a rocky road. Their culturing conditions can also vary per herb however don't worry–we're here to help!

Here are some essential advices for indoor gardening with vegetables. We'll focus on soil, light, and water.

You can must a potting mix instead of garden soil to ensure vegetables culture goodly inside. Choose the container based on the plant.

You also must to make sure that there is good drainage to avoid rotting the roots.

Important: Light is where these vegetables get finicky. They usually must 14-16 hours of light for best results, so putting them near windows might not be enough.

You can must to invest in culture lights for your vegetables to culture in tip-top shape inside.

Supposing you want to keep things simple, here's a popular indoor gardening idea for an endless supply of onion greens.

With a PET bottle and a several onions, you could culture your own self-contained onion greens in a harvest-friendly form. Cut the greens and allow this culture again when a while!

That said, indoor gardening with vegetables works best when you have culture lights. Since vegetables require much more sun than herbs, keeping them under the light is pretty much the only option.

Indoor Gardening Supplies

Indoor gardening is more than the herbs that you grow; this also includes the things you must to make that experience fruitful! Here are some essential supplies we recommend.

Culture Lights

Culture lights are artificial light sources that complement or completely replace the must for the natural sun.

They make indoor gardening possible and allow you to control the type and amount of light to stimulate growth in herbs.

Window Garden Kits

One of the easiest ways to get started with indoor gardening is to culture herbs on the windowsill.

Use pots that you already have or choose a space-efficient window garden kit.

Hydroponic Indoor Gardening System

Supposing you want a non-fussy indoor yard, consider a soil-free indoor gardening systems equipped with built-in culture lights, monitoring sensors, and a water reservoir.

This sort of system provides optimal culturing conditions for your herbs, letting you culture them in- and off-season.

It does take some of the craft of gardening away, however supposing you are often too busy to yard, this could be a good alternative.

Indoor Gardening Frequently Asked Questions

Here are some frequently asked indoor gardening questions that we thought we should answer. We hope you can find the answers useful.

Is indoor gardening hard?

Indoor gardening is what you make it. Supposing you want to have an easy-to-maintain yard, you can choose herbs and arrangements that are simple and not time-consuming.

May you implement indoor gardening with a vegetable garden?

Yes, you can culture lots of vegetables indoors. You must make sure that you have the right lighting, temperature, and nutrients in order for your herbs to do well, though.

When may I start indoor gardening?

There is no must to wait. With the right equipment and knowledge, you can start an indoor garden at any time of the year. In fact, you can even start gardens inside and move them outdoors later. Check our indoor gardening advices to get started.

Final Thoughts on Indoor Gardening

Indoor gardening possibly a fun hobby, a way to culture your own food, a simple way to add more greenery to your space, or a combination of these.

You don't must any experience as a gardener to get started with indoor gardening. this can be in itself a learning experience, however as you've gone past the preparation stage, you can have a goodr home and gardening skills to boot.

We say **lose no time and get started with indoor gardening**. You can enjoy the entire process and become a calmer, more mindful person as you tend to your herbs.

Made in the USA
Monee, IL
22 April 2021